G000045507

Catholics and Our Common Home

Caring for the planet we share

by
Sr Margaret Atkins CRSA

All booklets are published thanks to the generous support of the members of the Catholic Truth Society

CATHOLIC TRUTH SOCIETY

PUBLISHERS TO THE HOLY SEE

Contents

Acknowledgements

I am very grateful in particular to James Atkins, Paul Kelly, Margaret McSherry, Trish Sandbach, Mark Spalding, Fr Gerard Hanion and Ellen Teague for help and advice with revising this booklet, a version of which first appeared in 1995. Thanks are due to the John Bradburne Memorial Society and to Sr Mary Stephen Astley for permission to reproduce the poems 'Creation's Shapes' from *Birds, Bees & Beasts* (JMBS, 2007), and 'Lachrymae Rerum' from *The Trouble with NOT Writing Poetry* (Amor Deus, 2015).

ISBN 978 1 78469 086 1

Introduction

The priest, eighty looking like forty, gentle and humorous, had been telling us of his life as a missionary among the people of the Peruvian jungle. Oil had been discovered there in the 1970s and one day he was asked to go to the oilfield to say Mass for the workers. He was then invited to visit one of the 'batteries', as the drilling stations are called. They flew there by helicopter, over a vast carpet of trees, spreading in every direction. The priest knew that the rainforest below was alive with the colours, sounds and scents of a million species of plants and trees, birds, animals and insects. A group of air-conditioned cabins housed the workers but the forest wall surrounded them; they were in the middle of Peru's largest, and pristine, nature reserve.

One afternoon a couple of friendly engineers asked him if he would like to 'go for a walk'. This consisted of balancing on rusting pipes over acres of sludge surrounded by thousands of dead palms inhabited now only by parrots and macaws, making 'a horrendous racket', as the priest put it. His companions explained that salt water comes up with the crude oil and kills the vegetation. He asked if they were going to clear up the mess when the oil ran out. They replied, 'There is no money for that.' After the company left, it would be impossible for life to return. There would be nothing except the sludge and the dead trees - and the massive rusty wrecks of abandoned machinery. The priest was describing something shocking, but far from exceptional. This is how they - this is how many of us - regularly go about our business.

Threatened species: Bengal Tiger painted by Szabolcs Kókay.

Ecology and the Catholic Faith

Pope Benedict XVI said in his inaugural homily, 'The external deserts in the world are growing, because the internal deserts have become so vast.' His successor commented on this in his first encyclical, *Laudato Si' (LS)*:

> 'For this reason, the ecological crisis is also a summons to profound interior conversion. It must be said that some committed and prayerful Christians, with the excuse of realism and pragmatism, tend to ridicule expressions of concern for the environment. Others are passive; they choose not to change their habits and thus become inconsistent. So what they all need is an "ecological conversion", whereby the effects of their encounter with Jesus Christ become evident in their relationship with the world around them. Living our vocation to be protectors of God's handiwork is essential to a life of virtue; it is not an optional or a secondary aspect of our Christian experience' (217).

In relation to the environment, Pope Francis identifies two groups of Catholics: the critical and the indifferent. A third group might consist of those who are willing, even enthusiastic, but who feel discouraged about the possibility of making any real difference. This booklet tries to say something to all three: to challenge the first, to stir up the second, and to encourage the third! Its three sections will:

1. Show how basic elements of the Church's tradition mean that caring for creation is as central to our faith as, say, peace or justice.

2. Provide a guide to and selections from papal teaching in this area, including the recent encyclical.

3. Suggest how our faith can help us to close the gap between theory and practice in this area.

Science and fact

This is not the place to examine the scientific evidence for there being an ecological crisis. There is some controversy about the details of climate change, but even granting that, it is clear that there are enormous problems. We know that the extinction of all kinds of species, the destruction of a vast range of habitats, soil erosion and the loss of topsoil, the pollution of the oceans and the disappearance of marine life, are all continuing at a pace unprecedented since the human race began. Both detailed expert studies and ordinary human experience all over the planet tell us that this is so. Most of this can be traced directly and very obviously to the way human beings live their lives. But given that this is the case, what is its significance for those who profess the Catholic faith?

Fusiliers and other fish crowding over a coral reef in the Indian Ocean.

Consider four sets of facts and figures. Since 1980, about one fifth of the world's coral reefs have been destroyed and another fifth badly degraded;[1] average Arctic temperatures have increased at almost twice the global average rate in the past 100 years;[2] the world's richest countries make up 20% of global population but use 45% of all meat, 58% of energy, 84% of paper and 87% of vehicles;[3] roughly one third of food produced for human consumption is lost or wasted globally - about 1.3 billion tonnes.[4] Statistics such as these may prompt us to ask questions. 'What is the connection between them?' 'Has biodiversity got anything to do with religion?' 'Ought I to think about climate change *because* I am a Christian?' 'Should I live a life of waste less *because* I go to Mass?' In other words, what has our faith got to do with the crisis of the environment? Once we remember that the world is not ours, but God's, we can begin to see the relations to each other, to us, and to our faith.

Creation in Scripture and Tradition

'The earth is the Lord's' (*Ps* 24(23):1)

'We believe in one God, the Father Almighty, maker of heaven and earth, of all things visible and invisible.' The first article of the Creed provides the basis for the Christian's attitude to creation. Before we say anything else about the world and the creatures in it, we confess that they are, in fact, created, that God intended them, fashioned them, and sustains their life and existence. If we wish to cooperate with the will of God, we have to respect his creation. Indeed, the world is his gift to us.

In response to the crisis, some people have argued that we need a new 'environmentally friendly' type of religion. Some have even argued that Christianity is to blame for our environmental problems. Others have responded by looking more carefully at what the Church has always taught about the created order, and have rediscovered the rich resources already there in our tradition. The Old and the New Testaments, the writings of the Church Fathers and the lives of many saints have recognised and celebrated the goodness and beauty of other creatures.

Creation in the Old Testament

The Bible opens with the words, 'In the beginning God

created the heavens and the earth' (*Gn* 1:1). Since early times, Christians have interpreted this in the light of the Trinity: the Father creating through his Word, the Son, in the Spirit. This provides the context for the whole story of God's relations with his creatures. As God makes each new thing, the writer comments: 'And God saw that it was good' (e.g. *Gn* 1:12). Finally, he concludes, 'And God saw everything that he made, and behold, it was very good' (*Gn* 1:31). If ever Christians have been tempted to see the world as a dark and difficult place, they have always been reminded by these words that creation is good, because that is how the loving Creator made it.

Every single species is valuable, but only human beings are described as being made 'in the image of God' (*Gn* 1:26), and they are to have 'dominion' over the other creatures. At times, some Christians have been tempted to treat this as a licence to treat other creatures in whatever way they wanted. However, such an interpretation would not fit well with the broader Old Testament understanding of how a ruler should exercise power. It is more biblical to understand 'dominion' as a *responsibility*. So, for example, at first, human beings, along with other animals, are to eat only plants (*Gn* 1:29). They were given permission to eat meat only after the flood, and then in a controlled way (*Gn* 9:2ff.). As Pope John Paul II put it, 'Adam and Eve were to have exercised their responsibility over the earth with wisdom and love.'

Leaving the Garden of Eden

Matters were made more complicated, however, by human sin. Genesis 2 and 3 explore this idea through the story of the Garden of Eden. The punishment of Adam and Eve changed their relationships with nature:

> 'Cursed is the ground because of you; in toil you shall eat of it all the days of your life; thorns and thistles it shall bring forth to you' (*Gn* 3:17-18).

The harmony of Eden, where Adam named the animals, was broken.

The story of Eden has been interpreted in many ways over the centuries. In the past, some commentators understood it literally, others as an allegory or parable. Modern scholars treat it as conveying theological rather than historical truths. Some have thought that only human beings are fallen, while the rest of nature remains just as good as it was. Others have argued that the pain and violence we see in the natural world is best explained by seeing other creatures as also affected by the Fall. When human beings are fully reconciled with God again, they will then become the means for restoring all of creation to peace and innocence.

Working the land

After the Fall, the story says, working on the land would be hard. This reflected the experience of the people of the Old Testament. They lived as farmers and herdsmen and knew how harsh such a life could be. The Jews were not sentimental about animals. They killed and ate many of them, some they sacrificed, others they regarded as unclean. However, as their lives were intimately involved with plants and animals, they were less tempted than we are to separate themselves from the rest of creation. They liked to use agricultural imagery, as when Isaiah likens Israel to a vine planted by God (*Is* 5:1ff.). Their religious laws included concern for their domestic animals: the ox and ass and cattle were not to work on the Sabbath (*Ex* 20:10; *Dt* 5:14). Every seventh year was to be a jubilee, in which the land was given a rest (*Lv* 25:2ff.).

An important theme in the Old Testament is the connection between the well-being of the political and the natural worlds. After the Flood God made a covenant with every living creature, marked by the rainbow (*Gn* 9:16). Psalm 72(71) celebrates the just king, and links his righteousness with peace and fertility. The Messiah promised in Isaiah 11, as the Christian tradition interprets it, is a ruler who will bring not only justice to the human world, but also peace with and in the world of nature:

'The wolf shall dwell with the lamb, and the leopard shall lie down with the kid, and the calf and the lion and the fatling together, and a little child shall lead them … They shall not hurt or destroy in all my holy mountain; for the earth shall be full of the knowledge of the Lord, as the waters cover the sea' (*Is* 11:6,9).

God and his creatures

The Psalms were the basic prayerbook of the Jewish people. They develop the theme of God's relation to all his creatures. Psalm 104(103) meditates at length on the way that God created all the parts of the earth, and continues to provide for every animal:

'The trees of the Lord are watered abundantly,
The cedars of Lebanon which he planted.
In them the birds build their nests ...
The high mountains are for the wild goats'

(Ps 104: 16,18).

The Psalms also celebrate the way that all created things glorify God simply by revealing his creative power:

'The heavens are telling the glory of God;
And the firmament proclaims his handiwork'

(Ps 19(18):1).

This idea explains why Hebrew poetry could call on the hills to 'sing for joy' *(Ps* 98(97):8). Similarly, in the book of Daniel, the three young men in the fiery furnace are represented as singing an extended hymn of praise which summons the heavenly bodies, the weather, the mountains and rivers, the fish, birds and animals, each in their turn to bless God *(Dn* 3:57ff. This text, which was later known as the *Benedicite,* from the Latin for 'Bless', became a regular part of the monastic office.[5])

The final line of the Book of Psalms sums up this spirit: 'Let everything that breathes praise the Lord!' (*Ps* 150:6).

Jesus and other creatures

The Old Testament sets the context for the New Testament. Jesus himself was brought up in rural Galilee, and his parables show his familiarity with the details of birds, plants and animals, orchards and pastures, methods of farming and hunting. We can imagine him as a child, learning, probably from his parents, to identify the trees which would provide wood for carpentry, or fruit for the table. He used his observations of the countryside to make precise theological points. He gave no teaching about our attitudes to other creatures; however, in his teaching about the kingdom of God he takes for granted two significant assumptions.

The first is that we should have compassion for animals. In this, Jesus's interpretation of Old Testament laws about animals is shared by some, but not all, of his contemporaries. So, for example, he assumes that the law prohibiting work on the Sabbath allows an exception for giving water to one's animals (cf. *Lk* 13:15). There even exists an apocryphal story from the early centuries in which Jesus rebukes a man for beating his donkey.[6] This shows at least how early Christians thought that he would have responded to such cruelty.

The second assumption, based especially on the Psalms, is that God's providential care extends to every single creature.

In Jesus's sermons, God provides for the ravens (*Lk* 12:24; cf. *Ps* 147:9, *Jb* 38:41), clothes the lilies (*Lk* 12:27), and notices the capture of every sparrow (*Mt* 10:29; *Lk* 12:6). Jesus takes for granted the Jewish belief that the Father cares for even the least significant of his creatures. Although he contrasts the value of human beings and other creatures, he always does so to argue that human beings are *even more* valuable, never to deny the value of birds or animals.

Jesus, like almost all of his fellow-Jews, almost certainly ate meat. For the vast majority, though, this was a rare event: the fatted calf, and even a lamb, was killed only for a communal celebration. The ritual killings incorporated a sense of reverence, and of thanksgiving: the lives of animals were not taken casually or thoughtlessly.

At peace with the animals

Jesus's mission was to inaugurate the kingdom of God. This would include reconciliation between human beings and wild animals, as imagined by Isaiah. Mark's version of the temptations in the wilderness includes the phrase, 'And he was with the wild animals' (*Mk* 1:13). The phrase contains only four words in Greek, but the vocabulary is very significant. It means that Jesus was living peaceably with those very animals that would not be at peace with human beings until God's reign had begun. (A similar point can be made about the miracle of the stilling of the storm (*Mk* 6:45-51).) This theme of the reconciliation of all creation reappears when St Paul is reported as not having been harmed by a snake that fastened on his hand (*Ac* 28:3-6).

Creation and redemption

As the early Christians reflected in the light of the resurrection on Jesus's relation with the Father, they began to realise that he was not only the Messiah. He was the 'Son' in a special sense; in some mysterious way, God was present on earth in him. When the Son, the Word of God, became flesh (*Jn* 1:14), the divine was intimately united with the world of creatures. The Word was the one 'through whom all things were made' (*Jn* 1:3; cf. *Col* 1:16). Unlike some other contemporary religions, Christianity refused to see God as being dishonoured by contact with living things; rather, they are honoured by their relationship with him.

Through the death and resurrection of Christ, and through the outpouring of his Spirit, the 'giver of life', other creatures are drawn also into the story of redemption. This affects not only humanity, but the whole of creation, as St Paul tells us: 'For in him all the fullness of God was pleased to dwell, and through him to reconcile to himself all things, whether on earth or in heaven, making peace by the blood of his cross' (*Col* 1:19-20); and again: 'the creation itself will be set free from its bondage to decay and obtain the glorious liberty of the children of God' (*Rm* 8:21).

Similarly, the end of the Book of Revelation describes the created order as renewed and restored: 'I saw a new heaven and a new earth' (*Rv* 21:l). The sea, which symbolises chaos and disorder, has passed away. The river and the tree from the story of Eden return to provide life, food and healing (*Rv* 22:lff.).

In keeping with this, Revelation also emphasises and reinterprets the theme of other creatures too giving God praise. The mysterious four which sing to the Lamb, the lion, the ox, the man and the eagle (*Rv* 4:6ff.), are plausibly interpreted as representing respectively wild animals, domestic animals, humanity and birds. They are chosen as the most regal, and perhaps the most combative, members of their group. In heaven, however, they live in harmony and their role is not to lead, but to give God praise on behalf of 'every creature in heaven and on earth and under the earth and in the sea', who themselves will eventually also worship the Lamb (*Rv* 5:13).

Creation in the Church's tradition

Theology develops as the faithful ponder the Scriptures and pose new questions: about Christ and the Trinity, about the Church and salvation, about practical ways of living. The Bible and the theological tradition have been primarily about not ecology, but God and his dealings with humanity. Yet in the past Christians have fruitfully brought new questions to the Bible - for example, whether slavery should be abolished. Scripture does not give a direct answer, but provides principles to enable us to think the issue through. The environmental crisis is something new in the history of the Church. We cannot expect St Augustine or St Thomas Aquinas to have written about tropical rainforests or global warming! However, over the centuries, Christians have built on Scripture to develop basic principles of thought and ways of living which can guide us in answering these questions. Often they have been responding to specific controversies, and that can also help us to see more clearly essential elements of the Church's tradition.

The significance of the Incarnation

Some early Christian groups, known as Gnostics, were embarrassed by the physical world and by the human body and thought them an obstacle to religion. They argued, for example, that the Son of God could not have been born in the normal human way, or died a normal human death. Like some important pagan thinkers who criticised the bodily resurrection, they saw our flesh as a prison, from which we need to escape.

In response, St Irenaeus made it clear that a careful reading of the Bible does not allow us to think in that way. 'The word became flesh': as a result, Christians must value matter. He argued that it was an essential part of being human to be made of that flesh which God had made out of mud (*Gn* 2:7) and which is shared by Christ. The ultimate purpose of God's creation is to bring his creatures, flesh and spirit, to the glory of the kingdom: our own resurrection, like Christ's, will be bodily. St Irenaeus sees creation and redemption as a continuous, unified, work of God. Related to this is his awareness of the union of the spiritual and physical worlds in the sacrament of the Eucharist. The sacraments place the use of matter at the centre of our redemption. In short, the incarnation means that we Christians can never distance ourselves from material existence in all its forms.

The handiwork of God

The first chapter of Genesis has been studied more often and more carefully by Christians than almost any other section of the Old Testament. This produced a tradition of commentaries on the story of the six days of creation. A fine early example of these comes from St Basil. He sees the craftsmanship of God in blades of grass, or swarming fish, or feeding swallows. He finds goodness in the *beauty* of creatures, in their *usefulness*, and in the wonderful *organisation* that enables them to live. He also sees the 'virtues' and 'vices' in the animal world as a source of moral lessons for us. To put it concisely, the cosmos is a 'school for learning about God' (*Hexaemeron* I.6.2).

The goodness of all creatures

As a young man, St Augustine had joined a sect called the Manichees. They explained the evils in the world by the idea that the Creator was a second, bad, God. They produced as evidence creatures like maggots and scorpions. St Augustine became disillusioned with their ideas, and after his conversion he spent a lot of time explaining where they had gone wrong. In fact, every single creature is good. 'I could speak at length in praise of the worm', he once wrote (*De Vera Religione* 77). If we looked at a carrot-fly or a lion and thought that it was something bad, that was because we did not understand it properly. Often we are unable to see the value of things clearly because of our human fears and desires. We need to see the scorpion's sting from the scorpion's point of view (something easier for us since the invention of wildlife documentaries!). In short, other creatures are valuable in themselves, and not only for the sake of human beings.

The love of animals

Everyone knows that St Francis loved animals and preached to the birds. What is less well known is that he followed a long tradition. There are literally hundreds of stories about monastic saints which testify to their love of, and friendship and cooperation with, animals. St Macarius, in the Egyptian desert, was visited by a mother hyena, who led him to her blind pup, which he healed for her. A similar story of a saint befriending an injured lion was regularly linked with St Jerome. St Cuthbert befriended the seals and otters on his Northumbrian seashore, while St Kevin was said to have refused to have a monastery built because it would have involved destroying the wild animals' habitat. There is even a notable twentieth-century example in John Bradburne, a lay Franciscan, born in England, who was murdered while caring for lepers in Zimbabwe. He had a close affinity particularly with birds and bees, and he celebrated them in many of his religious poems.[7]

Such saints have been seen as restoring by their sanctity the original harmony of the garden of Eden, when Adam befriended and named the animals. The details of the stories make it clear that they were also imitating Christ. They, too, were anticipating the kingdom of God by making peace with the wild creatures. In short, the lives

Stained glass of Saint Francis of Assisi, Porto Azzurro, Elba, Italy.

of the saints make it clear that kindness to animals is an integral part of Christian holiness.

The praise of God by, through and for creation

Most of the saints who were known for their love of animals lived in religious communities. Many of these were in the countryside, which would then have been alive with the sights and sounds of birds and animals. Such religious, who were daily singing the Psalms and the *Benedicite*, would naturally have heard the dawn chorus, for example, as praise of God. As St Francis put it explicitly: 'My brother birds, you should greatly praise your Creator and love him always.'[8]

Francis was followed by a great many Christian writers including Christopher Smart in his exuberant poem 'Rejoice in the Lamb', and the Jesuit priest Gerard Manley Hopkins, who wrote: 'The birds sing to him, the thunder speaks of his terror, the lion is like his strength, the sea is like his greatness, the honey is like his sweetness; they are something like him, they make him known, they tell of him, they give him glory.'[9] Similarly, the Japanese Bishops have spoken of 'each creature singing the hymn of its existence' to allow us to 'live joyfully in God's love and hope'.[10] In short, whenever we destroy other kinds of creature, we impoverish the praise that creation offers to God.

Hopkins' meditation recalls another earlier theme, that creatures point to their Creator. As St Augustine put it: 'their beauty is their confession' (*Sermon* 241.2). Patristic

Mosaic of San Clemente, Rome, showing the vine symbolising Christ's relationship with creation.

and medieval writers, like modern poets, were highly sensitive to symbols, and saw no sharp distinction between contemplating actual birds, animals and plants and seeing God's creative presence in them. They spoke of creation as 'The Book of Nature', a second source of Revelation along with Scripture.[11] Individual creatures were like letters in the book.

St Francis's 'Canticle of Brother Sun', from which *Laudato Si'* takes its title, can be interpreted either as calling on creation to praise God or as praising and thanking God *for* the sun, moon and other parts of his creation. This latter theme is echoed by many poets, for example Hopkins in his sonnet 'Pied Beauty', which begins 'Glory be to God for dappled things'. A similar sentiment is implicit whenever Christian artists portray in careful detail the beauties of the natural world. A fine example is the twelfth-century mosaic from the apse of the church of San Clemente in Rome, which portrays Christ as a vine, with a variety of different animals and birds in his branches.

Christian asceticism

So far we have explored elements of Christian theology which imply that we should value and care for the natural world. But how do we do this in practice? The primary threat to our environment today comes from the increasingly intensive way in which we exploit natural resources, whether fuel, land, water or individual living things. To put it simply, we need to learn to be content with less. It is here that the tradition of Christian asceticism can help.

In the early centuries many Christians lived simple and self-denying lives. They inherited from the Jews the practice of fasting twice a week, they sometimes abstained from meat or wine, and they shared their wealth with the poor. Over time a relatively strict Lenten observance developed. Some, particularly monks and nuns, were extremely ascetical, eating very little, or giving away all their possessions. Such simplicity was seen both as retraining disordered desires and as freeing the mind to focus on God. However, Christian asceticism has usually been marked by a certain moderation: St Augustine made sure that wine was provided for the sake of hospitality, while wise monastic guides tried to ensure that over-enthusiastic individuals did not go to extremes.

It is also important that Christian asceticism has been communal in form: it has embodied ways of living that most of the community can manage (with sensible exceptions for the sick and elderly). Lay people needed a certain standard of living to fulfil their roles in their families and society, but they were encouraged not to aim at luxurious living, and if they were rich, they should use their money for others.

Being temperate

Christian thinkers inherited from Classical thinkers the four cardinal virtues, and one of these is particularly relevant here. It is revealing that it is difficult to find a

word for it in English. The Latin for it is *temperantia*, and
it means 'having a disposition to desire pleasant things in
moderation, in a way suitable for health and well-being'.
Notice that it does not mean *not* enjoying good things, or
fighting against one's desires, like someone in a constant
battle to stay on a diet. It is not quite the same as 'self-
control' or even 'restraint'. 'Temperateness' might be
a good word for it. The temperate person doesn't desire
physical luxury or excessive possessions, but enjoys using
good things in a moderate way, with care, for appropriate
purposes. Christians could do this, because their goal in
life was not worldly success: by living with a higher world
in mind, they could tread lightly on this earth.

Some people have seen Christian 'other-worldliness' as
showing a contempt for creation, and sometimes there has
been truth in the charge. Some Christians also adopted a
Puritanism that seemed empty of joy. But true asceticism
involved a joyful appreciation of and gratitude for the gifts
of creation (think of the simple practice of saying grace
before a meal). As G.K. Chesterton put it, 'We should thank
God for beer and Burgundy by not drinking too much of
them.'[12] Christian ideals here contrast strikingly with the
thoughtless consumerism that is damaging our planet today.

Christian tradition

The Christian tradition is absolutely clear: every living
creature is good, brought into being and sustained in

existence by the Trinitarian God, its Creator. At the same time, the created order is totally dependent on its Creator. It is also flawed, damaged at least by the fallen behaviour of human beings. As such, it is in need of the redemption brought by and through Christ, in the Spirit.

We can make the mistake of not valuing the world enough; we can also make the mistake of thinking of it as divine. If it were divine, nothing about it would need to be changed. This point is also important for thinking seriously about environmental issues. It is because the world is good and beautiful that it needs conserving. But it is because it is flawed and dependent that it requires understanding, effort, discipline and self-sacrifice to conserve it (or, as the Christian would say, to co-operate with God in conserving it).

The creation is an ordered system, with different creatures playing different roles. Human beings, according to Scripture, are made in the image of God (*Gn* 1:26). This has often been misinterpreted as if it gives us a licence to use other creatures however we wish. This is to forget that we ourselves are creatures, bound by the laws of God's creation. The Father, in whose image we are made, and then remade through his Son in the Spirit, sustains in existence every sparrow. Our special gift is our capacity to imitate God in his understanding and his love, of himself, of other people and of the rest of the world. We have a special responsibility, both to learn and to act with wisdom and with compassion.

Freedom and responsibility

Some Christians talk of our calling to be wise 'stewards' of creation. Other Christian writers remind us that we must also leave space for some other animals to be wild, in the wilderness so beloved by the early monks. Yet others (especially in the Eastern Orthodox tradition) speak of humanity as 'priests' of creation, consciously articulating its hymn of praise. Others might emphasise our role as reconcilers and peace-makers within creation. The Church leaves us free to use any of these ways of expressing our unique role.

Our uniqueness itself is important for thinking about ecology. If we are arrogant about our human gifts, we will make the mistake of thinking that we can solve ecological problems with technical fixes alone. If we go to the other extreme and imagine that there is nothing unique about us, we will forget that we have responsibilities that creatures without our freedom cannot have.

In short, according to the vision of Christianity, it is true that we, along with all other creatures, are permitted to use the material world, including other living things, for serious needs. However, we never have a right to destroy any of it wantonly, or to misuse or waste its resources.

What do we know that is new?

The basics of our faith do not change, but as our knowledge of the world grows, we need to integrate new ideas with our faith and ask new questions of it. Although most of us have less direct experience of the natural world than our ancestors, in other ways we know far more about it. For example:

1. The work of Charles Darwin and his predecessors and successors has made it clear how much we share biologically with our fellow-creatures, and how complex and even intelligent their lives can be.

2. Modern biology has also discovered the extraordinary level of interdependence among living things, and the ecosystems they inhabit. Similarly we understand far better the interrelated systems of the weather, the soil, the forests and the oceans.

3. Although for many centuries human beings have been able to modify their environment, and have been aware of this, both the scale of change and our awareness of it have changed dramatically. We know now that we can and do destroy species and their habitats irrevocably at a quite unprecedented pace, that significant amounts of pollution travel across the globe, and that we are exhausting the supplies of many natural resources. The scientific consensus also tells us that human activity is leading to potentially catastrophic disturbances in the climate.

4. Christians have always prioritised care for the poor. What is new about the modern world is the extent of our understanding of the structures of poverty, and of the way in which the actions of the rich and powerful can harm

those who have little. In particular, this is clearly true of environmental questions: most ecological damage is caused by the wealthy, and those who suffer most and are most at risk are the poor, either because their land and livelihoods are directly threatened, or because they are less free to move to safer and unspoiled areas. The cultures and societies of indigenous people and of the rural poor are closely bound up with their natural environment, so that damage to this affects them very profoundly.

5. Our ancient and medieval forebears cared for the land in ways that seemed to them, and mostly were, sustainable. They did not need to worry about spoiling the world irreversibly for future generations. Although they did unknowingly exterminate some species of animals, birds and fish, they did not cause large-scale damage to the planet. We know today, however, that we are passing on a world that is in much poorer shape than the one we inherited, and that we are storing up potentially huge problems for our descendants.

To sum up, the Christian tradition teaches us that the created order is good and precious, that we are responsible for the way that we treat it, and that we ought to try to live simply. Our knowledge of science, economics and human society suggests how urgently, and broadly in what ways, we need to change our collective behaviour if we are to care for the world that God created.

Modern Church Teaching

What the Popes have said

The first reference to ecology in a papal document was in 1971, when Pope Paul VI wrote of our 'ill-considered exploitation of nature' and insisted that Christians should collaborate with others in taking responsibility for dealing with this (*Octagesima Adveniens* 21). Every Pope since then has repeatedly emphasised our duty to care for all of creation.

Pope St John Paul II in *Sollicitudo Rei Socialis* 34 (1987) showed how ecological considerations were integral to a full and appropriate understanding of human development. In *Centesimus Annus* 37 (1991), he linked ecological problems to consumerism.

His fullest statement on the subject was his message for the World Day of Peace in 1990, which is well worth reading in full. The conclusion is clear: responsibility for all the life on our planet is a moral issue, and should be made a priority. True peace cannot exist without respect for the integrity of creation: the world is interrelated at every level, and we need to live in solidarity, respecting the harmony and balance of the planet. We must seriously examine our style of life in the light of this issue. In short, 'An education in ecological responsibility is urgent.'

Like his predecessor, Pope Benedict XVI regularly introduced care for ecology into his sermons, talks and writings.[13] A particular theme of John Paul II's which he developed was that of 'human ecology': we cannot restore proper relations with the natural world unless we also have a healthy human society, as all aspects of our shared moral lives are interconnected. He also discussed environmental questions at length in *Caritas in Veritate* 48-51 (2009), significantly integrating them into his vision for a Christian economy.

Pope Francis

Pope Francis signalled by his choice of name that ecology would be an important theme of his papacy. In his inaugural homily, he said: 'The vocation of being a "protector" … means protecting all creation, the beauty of the created world, as the Book of Genesis tells us and as Saint Francis of Assisi showed us. It means respecting each of God's creatures and respecting the environment in which we live.'

Francis gave a clear summary of *Laudato Si'* in its introduction (15). It has six chapters, in which:

1. He draws together the results of scientific research to give an overview of key aspects of the present ecological crisis. These include climate change, water shortage and the pollution of the oceans, the loss of biodiversity, and breakdown and inequality in human society.

2. He considers principles from Scripture and the Christian theological tradition which underpin, make sense of, and unify concern for the natural world.

3. He examines the root of the present crisis in the mastery over nature that we have acquired through technology. This fails to respect the reality of things, and leads to a manipulative attitude to both human beings and other creatures. This attitude goes hand in hand with placing human beings rather than God at the centre, and with a selfish individualism that ignores moral constraints.

4. He outlines an understanding of ecology which integrates humanity, under God, with the rest of creation. All aspects of human life too need to be integrated - ecological, economic, social and cultural - and at every level from daily family life to global politics, including the needs of the poor and of future generations.

5. He proposes dialogue on practical questions in order to promote a new, ecologically healthy way of thinking and living: dialogue among nations and religions, on a global, national and local level, and among the different disciplines of ethics, politics, economics and the natural sciences.

6. He offers guidelines for an education in spirituality and ethics that will assist us, as individuals and as societies, in the 'ecological conversion' that we need. Such a conversion

will bring not only practical benefits, but true freedom, joy and peace, personally, socially and politically. It is rooted in the creative love of the Trinitarian God.

Themes of *Laudato Si'*

Francis also identifies several themes that recur in different contexts throughout the encyclical: 'the intimate relationship between the poor and the fragility of the planet, the conviction that everything in the world is connected, the critique of new paradigms and forms of power derived from technology, the call to seek other ways of understanding the economy and progress, the value proper to each creature, the human meaning of ecology, the need for forthright and honest debate, the serious responsibility of international and local policy, the throwaway culture and the proposal of a new lifestyle.' (*LS* 16)

Laudato Si' is deeply rooted in the Catholic tradition, and particularly in the teaching of recent popes. At the same time Francis emphasises and develops particular themes in striking and fresh ways. His two predecessors had stressed the need to integrate nature with human ecology. He now makes the theme of integration central: 'everything is interconnected' (70). Theologically, we can only think of ourselves truthfully in relation to God, Father, Son and Spirit, and to all his creatures. Creation, redemption and the restoration of the universe in God are part of one plan.

On the moral plane, justice, peace and ecological concern are intimately connected, so that all the relevant intellectual disciplines must be integrated. Socially, what we do as individuals and families, as members of schools and parishes, as workers in industry or in agriculture, as town planners and transport managers, as small shopkeepers or bosses of multinationals, as nations and as continents, are intimately interrelated. Our political, social, physical, moral and spiritual well-being are inseparable. Poor and rich, dead, living and unborn, in every part of the globe, we human beings, along with every other species, are one family, with a common Father.

Pope Francis's very method of writing bears witness to this solidarity. He not only cites his predecessors repeatedly, but quotes at length from the ecumenical Patriarch Bartholomew, and includes a mass of quotations from texts of bishops' conferences from all over the world. The experience of all of humanity is represented here.

Papal teaching therefore calls us clearly and forcefully to care for our world, and to restrain the individual and collective greed and negligence that lead us to do it harm. We have a duty to reflect on this teaching and act on it. We should also make it known to others.

Creation in the *Catechism*

The *Catechism of the Catholic Church* draws together some of the themes discussed above. It emphasises the

unity of creation and redemption as part of the single plan
of a loving God (paragraphs 282-289, especially 288). The
cosmos as a whole is destined to be transformed at the end
of time: the destiny of human beings is shared with the rest
of the visible world (1046-1047). The world as a whole was
made for the glory of God (293-294). Every part of it is an
object of his providential care (303); and we are his co-
workers in the process of creation (307). Each creature, in
its own particular nature, reflects the goodness of God and
his beauty (299, 339, 341). Creatures are interdependent
(340) and there exists 'a solidarity among all creatures'
(344). Consequently, we must have 'a religious respect for
the integrity of creation' (2415).

Although we may make use of other creatures for
necessary purposes (2417), we must do so 'within reason-
able limits', and remembering our duty of kindness to
animals (2416). In using other creatures we must notice
how this might affect the lives of other human beings, in
the present and future (2415). (The duty to treat creation
wisely is included under the general heading 'Thou shall
not steal'.) In short, 'Man must respect the particular
goodness of every creature, to avoid any disordered use
of things which would be in contempt of the Creator and
would bring disastrous consequences for human beings
and their environment' (339).

Paul VI to Francis in their own words

Sollicitudo Rei Socialis *(John Paul II, 1987)*

34. One cannot use with impunity the different categories of beings, whether living or inanimate - animals, plants, the natural elements - simply as one wishes, according to one's own economic needs … When it comes to the natural world, we are subject not only to biological laws but also to moral ones, which cannot be violated with impunity.

Peace with God the Creator, Peace with all of Creation *(John Paul II, Message for the World Day of Peace, 1990)*

When man turns his back on the Creator's plan, he provokes a disorder which has inevitable repercussions on the rest of the created order. If man is not at peace with God, then earth itself cannot be at peace: 'Therefore the land mourns and all who dwell in it languish, and also the beasts of the field and the birds of the air and even the fish of the sea are taken away' (*Ho* 4:3) …

The ecological crisis reveals the urgent moral need for a new solidarity, especially in relations between the developing nations and those that are highly industrialised. States must increasingly share responsibility, in complementary ways, for the promotion of a natural and social environment that is both peaceful and healthy. The newly industrialised States cannot, for example, be asked to apply restrictive environmental standards to their emerging industries unless the industrialised States first apply them within their own boundaries. At the same time, countries in the process of industrialisation are not morally free to repeat the errors made in the past by others, and recklessly continue to damage the environment through industrial pollutants, radical deforestation or unlimited exploitation of non-renewable resources ...

Modern society will find no solution to the ecological problem unless it takes a serious look at its life style. In many parts of the world society is given to instant gratification and consumerism while remaining indifferent to the damage which these cause ... Simplicity, moderation and discipline, as well as a spirit of sacrifice, must become a part of everyday life, lest all suffer the negative consequences of the careless habits of a few.

Centesimus Annus *(John Paul II, 1991)*

37. In his desire to have and to enjoy rather than to be and to grow, man consumes the resources of the earth and his own life in an excessive and disordered way. At the root of the senseless destruction of the natural environment lies an anthropological error, which unfortunately is widespread in our day. Man, who discovers his capacity to transform and in a certain sense create the world through his own work, forgets that this is always based on God's prior and original gift of the things that are. Man thinks that he can make arbitrary use of the earth, subjecting it without

Responsible transport and urban planning.

restraint to his will, as though it did not have its own requisites and a prior God-given purpose, which man can indeed develop but must not betray. Instead of carrying out his role as a co-operator with God in the work of creation, man sets himself up in place of God and thus ends up provoking a rebellion on the part of nature, which is more tyrannized than governed by him.

In all this, one notes first the poverty or narrowness of man's outlook, motivated as he is by a desire to possess things rather than to relate them to the truth, and lacking that disinterested, unselfish and aesthetic attitude that is born of wonder in the presence of being and of the beauty which enables one to see in visible things the message of the invisible God who created them. In this regard, humanity today must be conscious of its duties and obligations towards future generations.

Caritas in Veritate *(Benedict XVI, 2009)*

48. Today the subject of development is also closely related to the duties arising from *our relationship to the natural environment*. The environment is God's gift to everyone, and in our use of it we have a responsibility towards the poor, towards future generations and towards humanity as a whole … In nature, the believer recognizes the wonderful result of God's creative activity, which we may use responsibly to satisfy our legitimate needs, material or otherwise, while respecting the intrinsic balance of

creation. If this vision is lost, we end up either considering nature an untouchable taboo or, on the contrary, abusing it. Neither attitude is consonant with the Christian vision of nature as the fruit of God's creation.

Nature expresses a design of love and truth. It is prior to us, and it has been given to us by God as the setting for our life. Nature speaks to us of the Creator (cf. *Rom* 1:20) and his love for humanity.

50. Human beings legitimately exercise *a responsible stewardship over nature* ... On this earth there is room for everyone: here the entire human family must find the resources to live with dignity, through the help of nature itself - God's gift to his children ... We must recognize our grave duty to hand the earth on to future generations in such a condition that they too can worthily inhabit it and continue to cultivate it.

51. *The way humanity treats the environment influences the way it treats itself, and vice versa.* This invites contemporary society to a serious review of its life-style, which, in many parts of the world, is prone to hedonism and consumerism, regardless of their harmful consequences. What is needed is an effective shift in mentality which can lead to the adoption of *new life-styles* 'in which the quest for truth, beauty, goodness and communion with others for the sake of common growth are the factors which determine consumer choices, savings and investments'. (*Centesimus*

Annus 36) Every violation of solidarity and civic friendship harms the environment, just as environmental deterioration in turn upsets relations in society.

Laudato Si' *(Francis, 2015)*

12. Saint Francis, faithful to Scripture, invites us to see nature as a magnificent book in which God speaks to us and grants us a glimpse of his infinite beauty and goodness … Rather than a problem to be solved, the world is a joyful mystery to be contemplated with gladness and praise.

21. The earth, our home, is beginning to look more and more like an immense pile of filth. In many parts of the planet, the elderly lament that once beautiful landscapes are now covered with rubbish … 22. These problems are closely linked to a throwaway culture which affects the excluded just as it quickly reduces things to rubbish.

23. The climate is a common good, belonging to all and meant for all.

33. Each year sees the disappearance of thousands of plant and animal species which we will never know, which our children will never see, because they have been lost for ever … Because of us, thousands of species will no longer give glory to God by their very existence, nor convey their message to us.

34. The degree of human intervention, often in the service of business interests and consumerism, is actually making

our earth less rich and beautiful, ever more limited and grey, even as technological advances and consumer goods continue to abound limitlessly. We seem to think that we can substitute an irreplaceable and irretrievable beauty with something which we have created ourselves.

41. In tropical and subtropical seas, we find coral reefs comparable to the great forests on dry land, for they shelter approximately a million species, including fish, crabs, molluscs, sponges and algae. Many of the world's coral reefs are already barren or in a state of constant decline. 'Who turned the wonderworld of the seas into underwater cemeteries bereft of colour and life?' [14]

44. We were not meant to be inundated by cement, asphalt, glass and metal, and deprived of physical contact with nature.

A true ecological approach

45. Frequently, we find beautiful and carefully manicured green spaces in so-called 'safer' areas of cities, but not in the more hidden areas where the disposable of society live … 49. Many professionals, opinion makers, communications media and centres of power, being located in affluent urban areas, are far removed from the poor, with little direct contact with their problems … Today we have to realize that a true ecological approach always becomes a social approach; it must integrate questions of justice in debates on the environment, so as to hear both the cry of the earth and the cry of the poor … 50. 'Whenever food

is thrown out it is as if it were stolen from the table of the poor'.[15]

57. It is foreseeable that, once certain resources have been depleted, the scene will be set for new wars.

58. In some countries, there are positive examples of environmental improvement: rivers, polluted for decades, have been cleaned up; native woodlands have been restored; landscapes have been beautified thanks to environmental renewal projects; beautiful buildings have been erected; advances have been made in the production of non-polluting energy and in the improvement of public transportation. These achievements do not solve global problems, but they do show that men and women are still capable of intervening positively. For all our limitations, gestures of generosity, solidarity and care cannot but well up within us, since we were made for love.

67. We are not God. The earth was here before us and it has been given to us ... 75. The best way to restore men and women to their rightful place, putting an end to their claim to absolute dominion over the earth, is to speak once more of the figure of a Father who creates and who alone owns the world. Otherwise, human beings will always try to impose their own laws and interests on reality.

God's loving plan

76. In the Judaeo-Christian tradition, the word "creation" has a broader meaning than "nature", for it has to do with God's loving plan in which every creature has its own value and significance. Nature is usually seen as a system which can be studied, understood and controlled, whereas creation can only be understood as a gift from the outstretched hand of the Father of all, and as a reality illuminated by the love which calls us together into universal communion.

77. The universe did not emerge as the result of arbitrary omnipotence, a show of force or a desire for self-assertion. Creation is of the order of love … Every creature is thus the object of the Father's tenderness … 83. The ultimate purpose of other creatures is not to be found in us. Rather, all creatures are moving forward with us and through us towards a common point of arrival, which is God, in that transcendent fullness where the risen Christ embraces and illumines all things. Human beings, endowed with intelligence and love, and drawn by the fullness of Christ, are called to lead all creatures back to their Creator.

84. Our insistence that each human being is an image of God should not make us overlook the fact that each creature has its own purpose. None is superfluous. The entire material universe speaks of God's love, his boundless affection for us. Soil, water, mountains: everything is, as it were, a caress of God.

90. We fail to see that some are mired in desperate and degrading poverty, with no way out, while others have not the faintest idea of what to do with their possessions, vainly showing off their supposed superiority and leaving behind them so much waste which, if it were the case everywhere, would destroy the planet.

Collective good

91. A sense of deep communion with the rest of nature cannot be real if our hearts lack tenderness, compassion and concern for our fellow human beings ... 92. We have only one heart, and the same wretchedness which leads us to mistreat an animal will not be long in showing itself in our relationships with other people ... Everything is related, and we human beings are united as brothers and sisters on a wonderful pilgrimage, woven together by the love God has for each of his creatures and which also unites us in fond affection with brother sun, sister moon, brother river and mother earth ... 95. The natural environment is a collective good, the patrimony of all humanity and the responsibility of everyone. If we make something our own, it is only to administer it for the good of all.

97. The Lord was able to invite others to be attentive to the beauty that there is in the world because he himself was in constant touch with nature, lending it an attention full of fondness and wonder ... 100. The creatures of this world no longer appear to us under merely natural guise

because the risen One is mysteriously holding them to himself and directing them towards fullness as their end. The very flowers of the field and the birds which his human eyes contemplated and admired are now imbued with his radiant presence.

106. Men and women have constantly intervened in nature, but for a long time this meant being in tune with and respecting the possibilities offered by the things themselves. It was a matter of receiving what nature itself allowed, as if from its own hand. Now, by contrast, ... the relationship has become confrontational. This has made it easy to accept the idea of infinite or unlimited growth, which proves so attractive to economists, financiers and experts in technology. It is based on the lie that there is an infinite supply of the earth's goods, and this leads to the planet being squeezed dry beyond every limit.

Intergenerational solidarity

111. There needs to be a distinctive way of looking at things, a way of thinking, policies, an educational programme, a lifestyle and a spirituality which together generate resistance to the assault of the technocratic paradigm ... To seek only a technical remedy to each environmental problem which comes up is to separate what is in reality interconnected and to mask the true and deepest problems of the global system ... 117. When we fail to acknowledge as part of reality the worth of a poor person, a human

embryo, a person with disabilities - to offer just a few examples - it becomes difficult to hear the cry of nature itself; everything is connected … 159. Intergenerational solidarity is not optional, but rather a basic question of justice, since the world we have received also belongs to those who will follow us.

183. Environmental impact assessment should not come after the drawing up of a business proposition or the proposal of a particular policy, plan or programme. It should be part of the process from the beginning, and be carried out in a way which is interdisciplinary, transparent and free of all economic or political pressure.

189. The financial crisis of 2007-08 provided an opportunity to develop a new economy, more attentive to ethical principles, and new ways of regulating speculative financial practices and virtual wealth. But the response to the crisis did not include rethinking the outdated criteria which continue to rule the world … 190. We need to reject a magical conception of the market, which would suggest that problems can be solved simply by an increase in the profits of companies or individuals. Is it realistic to hope that those who are obsessed with maximizing profits will stop to reflect on the environmental damage which they will leave behind for future generations?

191. We need to grow in the conviction that a decrease in the pace of production and consumption can at times

give rise to another form of progress and development … 194. Put simply, it is a matter of redefining our notion of progress … 202. It is we human beings above all who need to change … 204. The emptier a person's heart is, the more he or she needs things to buy, own and consume.

All is not lost

205. All is not lost. Human beings, while capable of the worst, are also capable of rising above themselves, choosing again what is good, and making a new start, despite their mental and social conditioning … No system can completely suppress our openness to what is good, true and beautiful, or our God-given ability to respond to his grace at work deep in our hearts.

209. We are faced with an educational challenge … 211. Only by cultivating sound virtues will people be able to make a selfless ecological commitment … There is a nobility in the duty to care for creation through little daily actions, and it is wonderful how education can bring about real changes in lifestyle … Reusing something instead of immediately discarding it, when done for the right reasons, can be an act of love which expresses our own dignity.

214. It is my hope that our seminaries and houses of formation will provide an education in responsible simplicity of life, in grateful contemplation of God's world, and in concern for the needs of the poor and the protection of the environment.

222. Christian spirituality proposes an alternative understanding of the quality of life, and encourages a prophetic and contemplative lifestyle, one capable of deep enjoyment free of the obsession with consumption … A constant flood of new consumer goods can baffle the heart and prevent us from cherishing each thing and each moment … Christian spirituality proposes a growth marked by moderation and the capacity to be happy with little. It is a return to that simplicity which allows us to stop and appreciate the small things, to be grateful for the opportunities which life affords us, to be spiritually detached from what we possess, and not to succumb to sadness for what we lack.

Unfolding in God

225. Nature is filled with words of love, but how can we listen to them amid constant noise? … 226. We are speaking of an attitude of the heart, one which approaches life with serene attentiveness, which is capable of being fully present to someone without thinking of what comes next, which accepts each moment as a gift from God to be lived to the full.

233. The universe unfolds in God, who fills it completely. Hence, there is a mystical meaning to be found in a leaf, in a mountain trail, in a dewdrop, in a poor person's face … 236. The Eucharist joins heaven and earth; it embraces and penetrates all creation … 240. Everything is

interconnected, and this invites us to develop a spirituality of that global solidarity which flows from the mystery of the Trinity … 243. Eternal life will be a shared experience of awe, in which each creature, resplendently transfigured, will take its rightful place and have something to give those poor men and women who will have been liberated once and for all.

Living What We Believe

The difficulties

The ecological crisis creates a striking gap between our professed beliefs and ideals and our actual practice. In the richer countries, even the greenest person is, for example, pumping more than his or her fair share of carbon into the atmosphere. All of us want something to be done about it; yet it seems almost impossible to change our own lives in the way that would be necessary. First of all, then, it is worth trying to understand our difficulties a little better.

1. We often feel that we have very *little choice*: we are imprisoned by the practical structures, and by the social expectations, of our society. 'We would love to walk to work,' we say, 'but it would take too long.' 'I'd be delighted to eat less meat myself, but my family complain if they don't get their steak.'

2. We are bewildered by the sheer *scale and complexity* of the practical issues. They involve controversial questions in science, politics and economics, as well as ethics. Since it is very difficult for non-experts to assess the arguments, the whole topic can leave us feeling confused.

3. It is hard to grasp the *significance of our individual actions* in the context of the whole globe. On the one hand, it seems that our own lives hardly matter: surely it makes an infinitesimal difference whether or not *I* drive to the shops. On the other hand, every single thing we do has some effect; moreover, such effects are both unknowable and unlimited in their range. Every drop of water I drink, every strand of cotton that I wear, every word I write on my computer, affects the environment in some way.

4. It is easy to feel that whatever efforts we make will be *pointless*. The less optimistic analyses seem to suggest that it is too late to avoid ecological catastrophe - so why not just make the most of the time we have left?

5. The *effort and self-sacrifice* that environmental aware-ness involves can just seem too much to cope with.

We need to take such thoughts seriously, as their combined effect can be paralysing. As Catholics, we can respond by pointing to the providence of God, grace and the virtues, and the community of the Church.

Trust in God

If God is the Creator, continuously providing for all his creatures, the ultimate responsibility is not ours. We must do our best to cooperate with his purposes, but we do not need to panic or despair. God brings good even out of evil, and certainly out of our half-hearted and often muddled attempts to do our best. So *faith* allows us to live with *hope*. The third of the theological virtues, *charity* or *love*, is a gift from God, through the Holy Spirit, 'poured into our hearts' (*Rm* 5:5). This expands our hearts so that we can love what God loves. Growth in charity will make us more aware of and compassionate towards all his creatures. The giving of this gift is *grace*: another reason for hope rather than despair is that we are not left to our own resources. If we open ourselves to the power of God, he will work through us. Our response to this will be *joy* and *gratitude*. The more we notice, delight in and give thanks for the rest of God's creatures, the easier we will find it to live at peace with them.

Green virtues?

According to the Christian tradition, living virtuously is not just good for the planet, it is good for *us*. We really will flourish more as human beings if, for example, we are liberated from our slavery to the world of consumption. Practising the virtues is worthwhile whatever the state of the planet. However, some of the traditional virtues have acquired new importance and extra dimensions in the light of the ecological crisis.

We have already mentioned the unfashionable virtue of temperateness, which is closely related to moderation, frugality, simplicity, abstinence and self-restraint. If we are to live simply, we need to know what counts as simple.

We can borrow a helpful distinction from St Thomas Aquinas, between decent and luxurious living. As levels of consumption steadily rise, it becomes harder and harder for us to identify and acknowledge our excesses. To do so, we need to detach ourselves from the temptations of peer pressure, image and status, and from the imperative to increase our wealth. Relatedly, we need to challenge the pervasive myth that whenever 'standard of living' rises, people are better off. Of course this is true for the very poor; it is equally obviously untrue for the very rich. The hard question is: at what point does it cease to be true? In other words, where does luxury begin?

Practical wisdom is also important because 'green' living demands awareness and understanding. The Church cannot tell us *what* to think about scientific, political or practical questions, but it can tell us that we *should* think carefully about these. Ecological issues are often very complicated, and we will need experts to guide us. However, we ourselves need to make the effort to understand where the things we use come from and how they affect our environment. We also need wisdom to make judgements about priorities: the answers in this area are rarely black-and-white.

Progress in the virtues always takes time: we stumble, slip backwards, we try again. Christians are used to this experience, and should not be discouraged if it is also a part of good ecological living. We are also used to the need for *communities* of virtue.

The community of the Church

We need communities for at least three sorts of reason:

1. To *practise* the virtues. This is partly because the efforts of a few individuals make little difference. More importantly, ecological living requires the right structures, e.g. for recycling or transport. This is important at every level. The Church is a community of communities: families, monasteries, schools, parishes, dioceses. We can often work together through these. Through these we can also influence our wider communities to steer policy or regulations in a greener direction, at local, regional, national or international levels.

2. To *teach* the virtues. Communities that live simply, for example, pass on to their members a healthy interpretation of temperateness. It is through communities also that we teach our children to live well. Perhaps the biggest ecological challenge, one for families, schools and policy-makers especially, is to inspire the next generation to live more lightly on the planet.

3. To *encourage* the virtues, and give each other moral support. In particular, we need communities with clear and courageous leadership, of the sort that recent popes have given in this area. This leadership is needed at every level. Such communities can not only live well themselves, but also provide a witness to others. The community of the Church is strengthened in its unity

and moral growth by the sacraments. The Eucharist, the supreme sacrament of unity, in itself symbolises our dependence upon and union with the soil and other living things.

Hard questions

When a Pope speaks out on a controversial issue, there will inevitably be objections. For example:

(i) 'The Church is not an expert in science or politics. Therefore, it should not comment on ecological issues.'

The first sentence is true. All Christians must inform themselves and make their own judgements on disputed questions, based on the most reliable and impartial scientific evidence available. Indeed, the Catholic tradition has always greatly respected human reason. Catholics have a duty to take seriously not only the 'very solid scientific consensus' (*LS* 23) on climate change, but also the incontrovertible evidence of damage on a vast scale in other areas. The Church's role is to set out moral principles and encourage the faithful in their responsibilities.

Similarly with *politics*. The Church cannot tell us that we should vote for the Green Party, or for any other political party. In extreme circumstances it might counsel us *not* to vote for a party whose politics were seriously and unquestionably unjust. However, the leaders of the Church should teach us moral principles, and make clear obvious applications of them. In particular, they should point out goals, attitudes and methods that are incompatible with Christian ideals, and encourage those that correspond well with them. So, for example, the critique of unprincipled capitalism in *Laudato Si'* is firmly based on basic principles, for example, 'wealth should not allow people to be above the law', 'money should never be a primary and over-riding motive of human life', and 'the weaker members of society should be protected from harm'. Where there is room for debate about which methods will most effectively put good principles into practice, the Church claims no special expertise. The Pope thus encourages serious debate and action in response to the failures of the global financial system, but does not propose a specific remedy (*LS* ch. 5 section IV).

(ii) 'Reducing the human impact on the planet will prevent poorer countries from developing to the level of rich ones. The Church should support the poor, not hold them back.'

The second sentence is true. Indeed, *Laudato Si'* repeatedly insists on the interconnection between care for the planet and care for the poor.[16] The question is what counts as real wealth. The 'super-development' (*LS* 109) of the richest countries does not provide a good model for development even for the countries themselves. Here papal teaching is in clear agreement with many environmental organisations, and with experts who are searching for alternative models of economics, based on true well-being rather than financial figures. Wise development would enable very poor communities to live in ways that are healthy, secure and sustainable (indeed, the very poor often cannot afford to do this). At the same time it would enable the rich to reduce their dependence upon excessive consumption and to cease from damaging behaviour.

(iii) 'The planet cannot sustain ever-increasing numbers of human beings living as we do now. Therefore the refusal of the Catholic Church to support population control and its beliefs about family planning are dangerous.'

The first sentence is true. Indeed, the Church has recognised that some concern over the size of population is justified; but we must be careful not to see the issue too simplistically. Most importantly, we need again to distinguish different styles of life. To quote a major European publication from Friends of the Earth: 'On average, an inhabitant of North America consumes around 90 kilograms (kg) of resources each day. In Europe, consumption is around 45 kg per day, while in Africa people consume only around 10 kg per day.'[17] The politically enforced control of populations deprives human beings (usually the poor) of a fundamental freedom of family life. The choice to have smaller families properly belongs to parents not governments. But what matters far more than the absolute numbers of human beings is how they live. The most urgent need for preserving resources is not to limit the numbers of those who already live simply, but to encourage the rich to learn to be more thoughtful, more imaginative, more cooperative and less selfish in the way that they (that is, most of us) live their everyday lives. As Pope Francis puts it: 'To blame population growth instead of extreme and selective consumerism on the part of some is one way of refusing to face the issues' (*LS* 50).

It is unlikely at present that many non-believers will be persuaded to embrace the full Catholic teaching on family planning. However, it is also worth pointing out that the holism of, for example *Humanae Vitae* has much in common with broadly environmental attitudes, in particular in its respect for our natural biological rhythms and its preference for patient self-discipline over technological fixes. Again, though opposition to abortion is often seen as 'right-wing' and ecological concern as 'left-wing', in fact they are both rooted in reverence for the marvel and mystery of life, especially when it is vulnerable.

(iv) 'Human beings are more valuable than animals. If we are competing for resources, human interests should always come first. Therefore green concerns are misplaced.'

The first sentence is true. And there are indeed a few other species, such as viruses that cause illness, which compete directly with human well-being and which it seems we must eradicate. In most cases, however, it is possible to live our lives and allow other species space to live theirs. It becomes impossible if we insist on methods of agriculture and industry that aim at nothing but profit. Finding gentler ways of continuing modern society demands commitment, imagination and flexibility. Many people have already accepted the challenge so that fine examples of conservation and sustainable development, in architecture and town planning, industry and commerce, agriculture and fishing, for example, are available to be followed (see *LS* 58).

Neither 'right' nor 'left'

Those who attack papal teaching on ecological questions as 'too progressive' and those who attack it as 'too conservative' both tend to rely on a model of conflict between human beings and the rest of creation. An approach that is both more deeply Catholic and more deeply ecological emphasises harmony rather than conflict. It is true that we cannot live without using other creatures. In a fallen world, we must sometimes compete with them. But the redemption of our world has already begun. It is our task, trusting in the providence of God, Creator and Redeemer, to bring peace and heal divisions wherever we can, rather than perpetuate competition and destruction. Indeed, it is part of God's providence that living reverent and simple lives will not only give other creatures room to live, but give us a cleaner, safer and more beautiful environment, reduce divisions between rich and poor, save time and money, improve our physical and mental health, encourage political peace, and provide more justly for future generations.

Practical suggestions

Fundamentally, there are only two ways in which we affect the rest of creation: by what we use, and by what we throw away. The basic rule of greener living is simple: think about those two things. But we need to do this in all contexts: at home, at school or at work, when we eat, travel, shop, build or vote. The Church has no special answers to the practical questions here. But it does encourage us to ask the appropriate questions. The checklist below might be a helpful aid to an examination of conscience in this area. It could be applied to individuals, families, schools, parishes or workplaces. Of course we should not aim simply to be able to tick off the checklist, but rather to internalise the virtuous attitudes and practices, in particular the attentiveness, that might correspond to it.

Praise for creation

- Do you notice, and give thanks and praise to God for, the beauty of the natural world?
- Are you are aware of and grateful for the animals, plants, land, sea and air that keep you alive?

Solar panels in the Vatican.

- Do you say grace before meals?
- Are you mindful of those who have no access to green spaces, or who are suffering from environmental disasters?

Live simply

- Could you live more simply?
- Could you waste less food or water, reuse more, recycle more, compost more?
- Do you sometimes abstain from unnecessary food, or eat fewer animal products?
- Do you buy things because you need them or because you want them?
- Could you choose greener products: more local, organic, animal-friendly, energy-efficient, durable?

Energy usage

- Could you turn down the heating, fill the kettle less, improve your insulation, or save energy in other ways?
- Could you choose a greener source or supplier of energy?
- Could you walk, cycle, or use public transport instead of the car? Need you fly?
- What kind of holidays do you choose?

Workplace and the environment

- How green is your workplace?
- How carefully do you dispose of potentially polluting waste?

- How well informed are you about sustainable methods in your area of work?
- Do you use your imagination to think of better ways of doing things?

Money and property

- How do you use spare land - gardens, churchyards, etc.? Can you encourage wildlife?
- How is your money invested?
- What is the carbon footprint of your family, school, parish, business?

Taking responsibility

- How well informed are you on issues such as climate change, GM crops, fracking, alternative energy, local building or transport plans?
- Are you really open to expert evidence on such questions, or do you allow your political beliefs to prejudice your judgements?
- How seriously do you take your political responsibilities, whether voting or engaging with public authorities?
- Do you reflect on the ways in which ecological damage might affect the poor?
- Do you reflect on your responsibilities to future generations?

Prayers and liturgy

As Christians, we naturally express our gratitude and joy for the order of creation in prayer. Before eating, we pause to give thanks for our food. Similarly, we may pause to appreciate and thank God for the air, the water, the soil, the plants, and the animals that keep us alive, beautify our world, and glorify God by their existence. We may pray in our own words, or use the words of Scripture, for example, Psalm 148:7-13:

Praise the LORD from the earth,
you sea monsters and all deeps,
fire and hail, snow and frost,
stormy wind fulfilling his command!

Mountains and all hills,
fruit trees and all cedars!
Beasts and all cattle,
creeping things and flying birds!

Kings of the earth and all peoples,
princes and all rulers of the earth!
Young men and maidens together,
old men and children!

Let them praise the name of the LORD,
for his name alone is exalted;
his glory is above earth and heaven.

Other useful texts for prayer or meditation include those mentioned above in the sections on creation in the Old and New Testaments.

The Church has not yet provided a Mass of thanksgiving specifically for creation, but the new Missal includes texts relating to times of seed-planting and harvest, and to various weather conditions, which could be prayed in this context. The *Book of Blessings* contains some lovely readings and prayers written for blessing animals, fields and flocks, and seeds for planting, and for thanksgiving for the harvest. Laudato Si' itself ends with two prayers, one usable by all believers in God, one specifically Christian. Other suggestions can be found in the bibliography at the end of this booklet.

Patrons of ecology

St Francis is well known as a patron saint of ecology, proclaimed by John Paul II. Less well known is Blessed Kateri Tekakwitha, a Native American saint, who shares this role with him. Unofficial patron saints of animals and the natural world might include those mentioned on p. 20 above, along with other popular saints such as Martin de Porres and Cuthbert, both great lovers of animals. One of the Church's greatest women philosophers, St Teresa Benedicta of the Cross (Edith Stein), wrote profoundly on the theology of creation. Many modern Christians have shown heroic courage in defending threatened habitats and the poor whose livelihood depends on them; an outstanding example is Sr Dorothy Stang, who devoted her life to working for and defending the rural poor in the Brazilian Amazon forest, and who was murdered in 2005.[18]

Finally, there are a wealth of poems which could be used to meditate on God's presence in and with his creation. Those of Gerard Manley Hopkins are well known, including 'God's Grandeur', 'Pied Beauty', 'Spring', 'Inversnaid' and 'Binsey Poplars'. Kathleen Raine's 'Word Made Flesh' meditates on the mystery of the presence of the Word of God in creation. W.H. Auden's 'Anthem' praises God for the ordered beauty of the world. Gwendy Caroe's lovely 'Touching Beauty's Hand' compares the failure to see God in the natural world to the failure to recognise Christ in Galilee. All of these are available online. The following two poems, which are less widely known, provide an appropriate conclusion, capturing the mystery of God's beauty reflected in his creatures.

Creation's Shapes

The sentient stars
Like silvery cars
Shall speed thro' space
The Lord to bribe
That He inscribe
In Heaven's book
Earth's every tribe
Both beetles, snakes
And mallard drakes
And dragon flies,

And every size
Of wingèd thing:
So shall they all
Make madrigal
For Christ the King.

John Bradburne (1921-79)

Lachrymae Rerum

For all this beauty too much sadness won
Weeps all in gilded tears over the bay.
Tears of things laced in the netted sun
Sapphire to king's royal lapping away
Into pale, frail, birdshell blue.
And the pearl and feel nearly of water
Sounds and rounds us, eddies us up to you,
Our world's steerer, the wild sea's Master.

Not only cormorant and gull glory and glide
Though, hover and dive the waves under,
Our eyes lustre or heart's hurt
Heal, quite caught in this world's wonder.
King, tender of birdsong and trees
What God but you weds to such earth such seas!

Sr Mary Stephen Astley (b. 1936)

Bibliography and Resources

For an introduction to the scientific issues:

Mark Maslin, *Climate Change: A Very Short Introduction* (Oxford, 2014);

John Spicer, *Biodiversity: A Beginner's Guide* (Oneworld Publications, 2012).

Alastair McIntosh, *Hell and High Water: Climate Change, Hope and the Human Condition* (Birlinn, 2008) interrelates science, ethics and culture.

For historical background:

Clarence J. Glacken, *Traces on the Rhodian Shore* (University of California Press, 1967, reprinted 1990): a fascinating and learned account of Western attitudes to nature throughout history.

Two important books from the early years of environmentalism were Rachel Carson, *Silent Spring* (1962, republished Mariner Books 2002) and Aldo Leopold, *A Sand County Almanac* (1949, republished OUP 1968).

For theological resources:

http://www.secondspring.co.uk/economy/ecology_environmen_ sustainability.html

On biblical themes: Robert Murray SJ, *The Cosmic Covenant* (Sheed and Ward 1992, reprinted First Georgia Press, 2007) and Richard Bauckham, *Living with Other Creatures: Green Exegesis and Theology* (Paternoster Press, 2012).

C. Derrick, *The Delicate Creation: Towards a Theology of the Environment* (Devin-Adair Company, 1972): a prophetic critique of the 'Manichee' tendency to distrust the created world.

Sean McDonagh SSC: several books, including *To Care for the Earth* (Geoffrey Chapman, 1986). A former missionary in the Philippines, he emphasises in particular the needs of the poor.

Celia Deane-Drummond, *Seeds of Hope: Facing the Challenge of Climate Justice* (CAFOD, 2009).

On animals: Helen Waddell, *Beasts and Saints* (1934, now available on

Kindle): medieval stories, illustrated with wood-cuts. Deborah Jones, *The School of Compassion: A Roman Catholic Theology of Animals* (Gracewing, 2009), explores the possibilities of developing the Catholic tradition of compassion for animals.

On 'green' virtues: see Margaret Atkins, 'Passenger Pigeons and Polar Bears: the Ethics of Global Warming', *http://www.thinkingfaith.org/articles/20080128_1.htm*, and 'Temperateness, justice and chocolate' (*Priests and People,* October 2003), reproduced at *http://jerichotree.com*

For summaries of and reactions to *Laudato Si'*:

http://jerichotree.com/2015/06/18/laudato-si-a-summary-of-pope-franciss-sweeping-eco-encyclical/

For a study and action guide: *http://columbans.co.uk/wp-content/uploads/2015/07/Laudato-Si-Study-and-Action-Guide-by-JPIC-Britain.pdf*

For ideas for prayer and liturgy:

CAFOD, *http://www.cafod.org.uk/Pray*

Between the Flood and the Rainbow (see below)

Ecumenical prayer resources: *http://www.ecen.org content/liturgy*

For practical advice on greener living:

http://www.greenguide.co.uk/ and *How Bad are Bananas? The Carbon Footprint of Everything* (Profile Books, 2010) by Mike Berners-Lee.

Get involved: ideas for what you can do as individuals and as parishes:

Between the Flood and the Rainbow, http://www.catholic-ew.org.uk/Catholic-News-Media-Library/Archive-Media-Assets/Files/Environment/Between-the-Flood-and-the-Rainbow

Global Catholic Climate Change, *http://catholicclimate movement.global/*

CAFOD Live Simply campaign, *http://livesimplyaward.org.uk/*

Eco-Congregation, *http://www.ecocongregation.org/*

Green Christian, *http://www.greenchristian.org.uk/*

Endnotes

[1] Spicer, *Biodiversity*, p. 91.

[2] *https://www.ipcc.ch/publications_and_data/ar4/syr/en/mains1.html*.

[3] *https://www.facingthefuture.org/IssuesSolutions/ConsumptionWaste/ConsumptionFastFacts/tabid/176/*

[4] *http://www.fao.org/docrep/014/mb060e.pdf*.

[5] It was, however, omitted from Protestant versions of the Bible.

[6] See Bauckham, *Living with Other Creatures*, p. 86.

[7] For more on John Bradburne, see *http://www.johnbradburne.com*.

[8] Thomas of Celano, *Life of St Francis*, ch XXI.

[9] 'On the Principle or Foundation', in Gerard Manley Hopkins, *Selected Prose* (OUP 1980) p. 108.

[10] *Reverence for Life. A Message for the Twenty-First Century* (1 January 2000), 89 (quoted in *LS* 85).

[11] Glacken, *Traces*, pp. 203-205. For a rich contemporary exploration of this theme, see Mary Taylor 'Faith is Obvious: the Apologetics of Creation', *Communio* 41 (Spring 2014).

[12] *Orthodoxy*, Fontana 1961, p. 64.

[13] See the collection *The Garden of God: Towards a Human Ecology* (CUA Press 2012).

[14] Catholic Bishops' Conference of the Philippines, Pastoral Letter *What is Happening to our Beautiful Land?* (29 January 1988).

[15] *Catechesis* (5 June 2013): *Insegnamenti* 1/1 (2013), 280.

[16] For a similar approach from a leading secular environmental group see an important report by Friends of the Earth, n. 17 below.

[17] *http://www.foe.co.uk/sites/default/files/downloads/overconsumption.pdf*.

[18] *http://www.sndden.org/en/who-we-are/where-we-are/latin-america/the-amazing-grace-of-sr-dorothy-stang*.